Preparing
FOR HARVEST

Preparing FOR HARVEST

JERRY WALKER

J. Kenkade
PUBLISHING®

Little Rock, Arkansas

J. Kenkade Publishing
6104 Forbing Rd
Little Rock, AR 72209
www.jkenkade.com
Facebook.com/JKenkade

The J. Kenkade Publishing name and logo
are trademarks of J. Kenkade Publishing, LLC.

Printed in the United States of America
ISBN 978-1-944486-73-0

Contents

Acknowledgments

This book was birthed from a place of desperation. I want to take this opportunity to publicly thank those that played a role for my hunger and challenged my thinking.

To my mom Wendy Young,
Your prayer life inspired me growing up. It inspired me to develop a closer relationship with God, myself, and to not make any decisions without seeking His approval first. Thank you!

To the man I share the name Jerry Lee Walker with,
My dad-Thank you for being courageous, strong, and perseverant. Watching you endure many setbacks and difficulties has been the reason for my tenacity and drive. Once more, thank you!

Apostle C.A. Turner,
Thank you for empowering me to go out to empower others. Being under your leadership has sent me into heights that the average person doesn't get to visit. Your commitment to God's people has astounded me and if I could be half the leader you are, I believe I'll be ok. Thank you!

Introduction

God the Father wants you to live an extraordinary life. It is His will for you. As a follower of Jesus Christ, you can live a quality life that is mind blowing. To live this quality life, it takes cooperation on your part. You must do the work. No one else can do it for you. Not your family, not your friends—not the pastor, not the therapists…YOU! They can give you advice and knowledge, but you still must apply. A great part of you doing the work is taking responsibility for your life which is owning it. When you begin to take ownership or responsibility, you now become sensitive to where God is leading you. The very fact that you are reading this tells me that you are at the place of accepting responsibility for your life.

There are **7 Guidelines** that are critical to your success at taking ownership of your life:
  Stop Blaming
  Forgive
  Change Your Attitude
  Decide What You Want
  Become Intentional
  Compete With No One
  Check-in With Yourself

These guidelines are what the 31-day journey is all about. I'm not selling you a quick fix, but I am providing a place to start.

I want to challenge you each morning when you get up to take some time out before checking emails, social media, or the news. Delegate that time to getting into God's presence and allowing it to dwell with you throughout your day.

Read the devotional for that day. I've left space for you to use to make notes, to plan your day, and to analyze your thinking.

NOTES

Preparing FOR HARVEST

Day 1
How You Living?

Matthew 19:30
"Many that are first shall be last; and the last shall be first."

DO YOU EVER GET TIRED of doing the same things repeatedly, and getting the same results that are not benefiting to the person you want to become? Maybe you've been putting your flesh first and your spirit last, which causes destruction. Thank God for His goodness and mercy that no matter what we do, they will never leave our side. We could never repay God for His many gifts to us. A way that we show God that we are thankful for the things He has done is to put our *spirit* man before our *fleshly* man.

When you walk in the spirit, you won't fulfill the lusts of the flesh which is what Galatians 5:16 tells us. When walking in the spirit, you'll hear instruction that keeps you away from destruction.

We have been born with a sinful nature.

What this means is that our flesh has been first, but Matthew 19:30 helps us to understand the shift that's about to take place. We are spirits; when the flesh man dies, we will continue to live. Don't waste your days living as something you're not. You are a spirit on an assignment for the Kingdom of God who has a fleshly body to operate

legally in the earth realm.
    Follow God's plan and live your life as a spirit.

NOTES

JERRY WALKER

Day 2
Be Persuaded

Romans 8:38
"For I am persuaded, that neither death, nor life, nor angles, nor principalities, nor powers, nor things present, nor things to come, nor height, nor death, nor any other creature, shall be able to separate us from the love of God, which is in Christ Jesus our Lord."

PERSUASION IS A VERY powerful word. It's a mental acceptance that what I hear, read, dream, see, desire, and/or imagine is truth. So, Paul was telling us in Romans that he believed Christ and everything that He represents. Paul saw it as truth while others didn't even believe that Jesus was the son of God. This could be why Paul failed several times in his walk with God, but he maintained his persuasion that nothing could separate him from God's love. **Agape love:** the unconditional type of love.

You must be persuaded in your walk with God. There will be times when you may not make the best decisions and you will make choices outside the **Will of God**. It doesn't mean you're not saved, but it means you're more in touch with your natural man than your spiritual man at that moment. We are humans in need of a savior.

The biggest mistake that a **Child of God** can do is question their salvation and God's love for them.

Continue to believe in your heart and confess out of your mouth that you are saved. Live under the persuasion that Paul lived under which is that **NOTHING** can separate you from the *Love of God.*

NOTES

_____
_____
_____
_____
_____
_____
_____
_____
_____
_____
_____
_____
_____
_____
_____
_____
_____
_____
_____
_____
_____
_____
_____
_____
_____
_____
_____
_____
_____
_____
_____
_____

Day 3
Limitless God

Exodus 3:11-12
*"And Moses said unto God, who am I that I
should go unto Pharaoh, and that I should bring
forth the children of Israel out of Egypt? And
God said unto Moses, I AM THAT I AM: and
He said: Thus, shalt thou say unto the children of
Israel, I AM hath sent me unto you."*

IN THIS SCRIPTURE, God is telling us His ability because He didn't want to spend an eternity explaining who He was and what He could do. He simply called Himself "I AM". The fact that God called Himself "I AM" is a clear indicator that He can become whatever we need Him to become. If you need Him to provide, He will become **Jehovah-Jireh**. If you need Him to heal, He becomes **Jehovah-Rapha**. If you need peace, He becomes **Jehovah-Shalom**. The lists of Gods names go on and on because He is limitless! Acknowledge God for being who He is in your life on today. Give thanks to Him and even share with Him what you need Him to become. He is the **Great I AM**. There is nothing too hard for God to do in your life. Many of you all have petitions before Him and He is well able to fulfill and deliver what it is that you desire of Him.

NOTES

Day 4
Preparation by God

Psalm 31:14-15
*"But I trusted in thee, O Lord: I said, Thou art
my God. My times are in thy hand...."*

IN A WORLD of immediate gratification, it is hard to
wait on God. We are the generation where we can make
things happen on our own, instantaneously. Waiting on
God means that we must be subject to His will even when
it's not the direction we want to go. God is a strategist, and
when we don't have something by the time we think we
should have it, it's because God sees some imperfection or
flaw that can cause us to lose our integrity and curse what
was meant to bless. Give up knowing: *when, how, where*
and *why* and take on the attitude that says, *"It's hard, but
I'm willing to learn how to trust you, dear God."* Let's start
today with having the faith that everything is going to work
together for an appointed time.

Remember that if you don't have something that you
think you should have such as the following: *a spouse,
promotion, house, car etc.*, God is allotting you this time to
prepare yourself for it.

Delay doesn't mean denied.
In due time you will have the desires of your heart.

NOTES

_____
_____
_____
_____
_____
_____
_____
_____
_____
_____
_____
_____
_____
_____
_____
_____
_____
_____
_____
_____
_____
_____
_____
_____
_____
_____
_____
_____

Day 5
Child of God

1 John 1:7
"But if we walk in the light, as He is in the light, we have fellowship one with another, and the blood of Jesus Christ His son cleanseth us from all sin."

BY TRUSTING IN GOD'S WORD, we become one with Him. By becoming one with Him, we are connected to love, peace, and happiness. God sent His son to wipe us from all of our sins and the only way to **receive** is to **believe** and walk in the *Word of God*. The word of God is His **Wisdom** and **Instruction** that brings light into darkness.

Today I challenge you to live a life as a ***Child of God***. Sons and daughters don't have to go through religious acts and traditional steps to engage in an intimate relationship with the Father.

By reading Gods word, believing His word, and walking in the light, you can have direct fellowship with God more intimate than ever before!

NOTES

_____
_____
_____
_____
_____
_____
_____
_____
_____
_____
_____
_____
_____
_____
_____
_____
_____
_____
_____
_____
_____
_____
_____
_____
_____
_____
_____
_____
_____
_____

Day 6
Intimacy with God

Matthew 22:37
"Thou shalt love the Lord thy God with all thy heart, and with all thy soul, and with all thy mind, and with all thy strength: this is the first commandment."

THE BEGINNING of your fresh start is an awesome time for you to engage in a deeper and more intimate relationship with God. So many things in life will come to try to weigh us down. Thank God for His grace that gives us strength and power to endure! I'm talking about the type of relationship that when the enemy comes in like a flood, it won't even be noticeable because of God's presence. Start your new, more profound relationship with God today.

I declare:

Increase in your life, increase in your prayer life,
increase in your fasting, increase in your giving,
and increase in your home.

God wants your time spent here on earth to be pleasurable, but you must be in relationship with Him to get order and instruction. To really understand intimacy, we must come to the realization that we need Him and He desires us. Yes, of course God desires you! That's the reason why He gave His only begotten son. It was a decision out of intimacy.

Here's a breakdown of the word intimacy: In-ti-ma-cy (In-To-Me-See). This means that true intimacy is being able to see the inside of the entity that you are intimate with— knowing God's heart and God knowing your heart.

NOTES

_____
_____
_____
_____
_____
_____
_____
_____
_____
_____
_____
_____
_____
_____
_____
_____
_____
_____
_____
_____
_____
_____
_____
_____
_____
_____
_____
_____

Day 7
Good Living

Ecclesiastes 3:12-13 (NLT)
*"So, I concluded there is nothing better than to
be happy and enjoy ourselves as long as we can
And people should eat and drink and enjoy the
fruits of their labor, for these are gifts from God."*

SOLOMON GIVES US great advice in this text. He is telling us to make the most out of our days—not in a materialistic, covetous way, but a spiritual way. We make the most out of our days by including God in all that we do and being joyful in His presence. God is in control of all. Our ups and our downs are orchestrated by heaven. Solomon tells us to enjoy the fruits of our labor. This is because so many people work all the time, but never take the time out to enjoy what they are working for.

My suggestion is that any bill that you have on anything that you are not enjoying, GET RID OF IT! You should enjoy the type of car you drive, house you live in, watch you wear, food you eat, etc. We are here only a moment and should enjoy every second of it. Again, the scripture refers to this as *"A Gift from God"*.

Ponder on this thought today: If you were to die today right this second, would you be able to say that you made the most out of your earthly experience? Would you be able to say God was with you in your decisions, on your job, interacting with your family, and just your day to day activities? Part of the Christian walk is us learning how to take a step back from the cares of the world and all its anxieties and just enjoy where we are.

This is a beautiful gift!

NOTES

JERRY WALKER

Day 8
The Lord's Dwelling Place

Joshua 24:15 (NKJV)
"If it seems evil unto you to serve the Lord,
choose you this day whom ye will serve; whether
the gods which your fathers served that were
on the other side of the flood, or the gods of the
Amorites, in whose land ye dwell: but as for me
and my house, we will serve the Lord."

WE LIVE IN A TIME where vanity has taken over making idols out of things that are perishable. Matthew 6:19-21 reads, "Do not lay up for yourselves treasures on earth, where moth and rust destroy and where thieves break in and steal, but lay up for yourselves treasures in heaven, where neither moth nor rust destroys and where thieves do not break in and steal. For where your treasure is, there your heart will be also."

While others are serving gods such as money, people, places, and things, you make a decision to serve the Lord.

Joshua said, "As for me and my house, we will serve the Lord" (Joshua 24:15).

Everything He was connected to had to serve the Lord. Why serve the creations when you can serve the Creator?

NOTES

_____
_____
_____
_____
_____
_____
_____
_____
_____
_____
_____
_____
_____
_____
_____
_____
_____
_____
_____
_____
_____
_____
_____
_____
_____
_____
_____
_____
_____

Day 9
Extension of Jesus

John 15:5
"I am the vine, ye are the branches: He that abideth in me, and I in him, the same bringeth forth much fruit: for without me ye can do nothing."

JESUS IS TELLING US that He is the *source* and we are the extension of the source. As the fruit that the source produces, we should be producing as well. *Love, Joy, Long-suffering, Gentleness, Goodness, Faith, Meekness, Temperance* are the fruit that we should be bringing forth being the extension of Christ. Without bearing these fruits, we can do nothing beneficial in the Kingdom of God.

Jesus is a man, therefore He needs an extension. He can only be in one place at one time. Christ means the anointed one. Therefore, God anoints His children. He anoints the man who has a sinful nature and sends him out to do the work that Jesus left off doing. So now people can experience the ministry of Jesus all around the world at the same time.

Be a branch today! Be the extended source! We are all here to work the works of Christ.

Paul says in Romans 12:3 not to think of ourselves more highly than we should, but to think soberly accordingly as God has dealt to every man the measure of faith. Although we are doing the work, it is Christ's spirit that is winning the souls.

NOTES

Day 10
The Simple Life

Proverbs 3:5
*"Trust in the Lord with all thine heart; and lean
not unto thine own understanding."*

IT IS EASY for us to make life more complicated than
God's original plan. The plan that God has created for our
lives is simple. Jeremiah 29:11 says, "For I know the plans I
have for you, declares the Lord, plans to give you hope and
a future."

Simple, right?

Prosperity, Hope and a Future.

The reason we fall into chaos is because we allow the
enemy to move us out of position so that we can't see the
salvation of the Lord. If we read and hear Gods word, it
builds our faith and trust. When God has our total trust,
doors open and life begins to flow. You don't have to
understand everything, but you are required to trust and
take God for His word.

With your own ability. You can only go so far. With
Divine help, you can save yourself headache, pain, turmoil,
and all those negative feelings that usually generate into
our reality. It is perfectly fine not to know everything. If we

knew everything, we wouldn't need a Higher Power.

Today I want you to let go and let flow! Trust God and simplify your life!

NOTES

Day 11
Live in the NOW!

Matthew 6:34
"So, do not worry or be anxious about tomorrow, for tomorrow will have worries and anxieties of its own. Sufficient for each day is its own trouble." **(AMPC)**

EACH DAY THAT YOU WAKE UP is full of promises that God wants you to receive. When you focus on the future more than you focus on the moment, you become blinded to what God wants you to have in the NOW! By keeping your mind focused on the *second*, the *minute*, and the *hour*, you have a more productive, effective, fulfilled, and positive day.

Take a moment and breathe in for three seconds and then out for five.

Feels good, right?

That's how you should go through your days feeling. You may be on the job, riding in the car, cooking, or walking the dog. No matter where you are or what you are doing, take a moment and breathe!

Enjoy your day at work, enjoy the ride home, enjoy cooking dinner for the family, enjoy walking the dog. So, often we miss God's presence because we have worries and anxieties about the future.

Relax! Take it a moment at a time.

NOTES

Day 12
Expect Nothing but Greatness

Proverbs 23:18
"... *thine expectation shall not be cut off.*"

I WOULD LIKE TO START OFF with a very powerful quote by Confucius: "He who says he can and he who says he can't, are both right." Whatever you expect, you are going to receive— curses or blessings.

IT'S LAW!

If you expect low, you get low. If you expect high, you get high. You see, your expectation gives you a quality life— low in caliber or high in caliber. God has given us free will. This means we can decide what to expect. Both heavenly and demonic forces are around us to see who we will give permission to operate in our lives.

To be a representation of Christ means that we should be expecting to be blessed: *the head and not the tail, the lender and not the borrower.*

The Holy Spirit is working to manifest God's perfect will. It is our expectations that give permission for the Holy

Spirit to work its works.

Have great expectation today!

God wants to bless you and all you need to receive it is have expectation. There are numerous people in the body of Christ that are expecting and planning for the worst. God has not given us the spirit of fear; it comes from the enemy.

Live a fearless life full of possibilities and opportunities for success.

Expect nothing but greatness!

NOTES

Day 13
Focus on the Positive

Philippians 4:8
*"Whatsoever things are true, whatsoever
things are honest, whatsoever things are pure,
whatsoever things are lovely, whatsoever things
are of good report; if there be any virtue, and if
there be any praise, think on these things."*

IT'S SO HARD TO FOCUS on the positive when we live
in a world that seems to be so negative and overtaken by
evil spirits. When you don't live in a place of positivity, you
can and will become *sick* and *unmotivated*.

Being **positive** reduces *blood pressure, gives your immune
system a boost, helps you cope with stress, gives you energy,
and it enhances your social life which is connected to longer
life*. I recommend that today you pull out your photo
album and reflect on those moments that you experienced
the most joy. Maybe it was your wedding, or the birth of a
child or maybe it was a birthday.

Whatever it is, take some time today and go back
and relive that moment. Reliving the positive moments
is a setup to creating more positive experiences.

NOTES

Day 14
Creating Positive Moments

Isaiah 43:19
"Behold, I will do a new thing; now It shall spring forth; shall ye not know it? I will even make a way in the wilderness, and rivers in the desert."

NEVER GET STUCK in memory lane. It's ok to go back and relive the past experiences to bring current joy as we did yesterday. My brothers and my sisters, God wants to do a new thing. No matter what you are going through, no matter your wilderness or desert, God will open a door for you to create another special moment. God understands that sadness, bitterness, and depression can keep you from Him. So, it is in His Fatherly duty to give you a life of *abundant joy, victory, and love.*

Today, look for an opportunity to create a new experience in your life! Don't be closed in and afraid to try new things. Try a new food, do a family activity, volunteer at a local church, or nonprofit organization. I found that I'm most happy when I'm giving. When are you most happy—unselfishly? Oh, and don't forget to take pictures for the photo album!

NOTES

JERRY WALKER

Day 15
Own Yourself

Ephesians 4:26-27
*"Be ye angry, and sin not: let not the sun go
down upon your wrath:
Neither give place to the devil"*

WHEN UNCONTROLLABLE life events happen, the mind and the emotions can get the best of us. Own Yourself! You rule you, not your mind and emotions. When you allow your mind and emotions to rule over you, you are a slave. The purpose of Jesus is to set us over into freedom. Freedom— not just from the enemy, but freedom from toxic thoughts and emotions.

Take custody of your soul again. Growing in God means learning how to respond to situations and not react to them.

When you respond wisely, there is a flow that causes less chaos in your life. Reacting to life's circumstances only makes things worse.

Possess your Soul and Own Yourself!

NOTES

Day 16
You Can Do It!

Luke 1:37
"For with God nothing shall be impossible."

THERE IS NOTHING too hard with God. When we think we can reach our fullest potential without Him, we are foolish. It is God that gives us the strength to do all that we do with integrity and excellence. When we disconnect from God, we are actually disconnecting from our strength. This is when we begin to be filled with *anxiety, frustration,* and *ultimately... depression.*

Luke 21:34 reads to be, "...Careful, or your hearts will be weighed down with carousing, drunkenness and the anxieties of life, and that day will close on you (depression) suddenly like a trap" (NIV). Proverbs 4:23 NIV tells us to "Guard your heart above all else, for it determines the course of life (the possible or impossible)".

Failure is not an option, therefore being away from God isn't an option. True success comes from a connection of man, and the supernatural power of God.

Walk with God and live successfully.

You can do it! You can reach every goal, accomplish every dream, and fulfill your purpose.

Don't be weary in the work of the Lord. God has a reward for those that diligently seek Him.

NOTES

Day 17
No More Mediocrity

1 Peter 4:1-2
"Forasmuch then as Christ hath suffered for us in the flesh, arm yourselves likewise with the same mind: for he that suffered in the flesh hath ceased from sin; that no longer should live the rest of his time in the flesh to the lusts of men, but to the Will of God."

IF YOU ARE A BORN-AGAIN BELIEVER, then you understand or should understand that the day you were born again, you died at the same time. You died to the lustful desires of the flesh, to lasciviousness, excess of wine, reveling, banqueting, and abominable idolatries. Now that we've walked away from these evil things, we take on the mind of Christ and walk into the will of God.

Today, walk in your new life of power, authority, and dominion. Take on the mind of Christ. Live your life the way the Creator intended: full of His presence, power, prosperity, and purpose.

Being a born-again believer means death to the flesh. Your new attributes consist of *love, patience, joy, peace, kindness, goodness, and faithfulness.*

NOTES

Day 18
Forget, Reach, Press

Philippians 3:13-14
"Brethren, I count not myself to have apprehended: but this one thing I do, forgetting those things which are behind, and reaching forth unto those things which are before, I press toward the mark for the prize of the high calling of God in Christ Jesus."

WHEN WE FOCUS on short-comings, failures, and wrong turns from the past, we become paralyzed. If we are going to do anything in and for the Kingdom of God, we must gain and keep our momentum. God's future for you is **NOT** filled with failures, short-comings, or wrong turns.

This future with God is full of success, excellence and opulence. It's filled with learning opportunities, chances for growth and you becoming a vessel used by the holy spirit.

Don't journal today without understanding that your past doesn't define you, or dictates your future.

There are countless people I could tell you about that have a horrible past, but extraordinary present lives.

The high calling of God is found in Jeremiah 29:11.

It's an urgent call, for it resuscitates you.

JERRY WALKER

NOTES

Preparing FOR HARVEST

Day 19
Leap of Faith

Matthew 9:29
"According to your faith be it unto you..."

FAITH IS A VERY POWERFUL TOOL. With faith, we can tell our lives to go in the direction of the will of God. Likewise, we can tell the traps of the enemy where to go.

Jesus tells us in Matthew 17:20, "If you have the faith the size of a mustard seed, you can speak to a mountain and tell it to move from here to there" (NIV).

What people can't figure out or accomplish, your faith will work it out.

"According to your faith be it unto you."

You can have what you say you shall have.

You can be what you say you shall be and you shall do what you say you shall do.

When you start confessing these affirmations, the miracle is that you begin to conduct yourself accordingly. With commitment and discipline, you can see a total life turn around.

Today is the day that you stretch your faith out further than you ever have. Notice I didn't say grow your faith.

The only requirement is a *mustard seed amount*. When you stretch your faith, you are willing to take *risks, face hardship, and endure the pain.*

It's time to bring out that business idea, non-profit venture, and it's time to write that book or start that album. Don't put your God given gifts and talents to the side. Write a plain vision that those that you come across (that I call divine connections) can run with and help you advance the Kingdom of God.

NOTES

Day 20
Receive Your Blessing

Haggai 2:19
"Is the seed yet in the barn? Yea, yet the vine,
and the fig tree, and the pomegranate, and the
olive tree, hath not brought forth: from this day, I
will bless you."

GOD WANTS TO BLESS YOU. It is a part of His will for your life to have His blessing. I would like to submit to you this day: **There is not a season, time, or turn to receive the blessings of the Lord.**

Today is the day!

By believing that God wants to bless you, you can open doors in every area of your life for goodness to flow.

Your commitment to God's word will prove to Him you can handle the blessing.

Today God will bless you!

Be positive and optimistic. Don't focus on what happens, but keep in mind the things that God is doing in the spirit. The times and seasons are in God's hand. It doesn't take years of process to get the materialization.

You are **BLESSED**! Now receive it!

NOTES

Day 21
Be Blessed

Psalm 1:1
"Blessed is the man that walketh not in the
counsel of the ungodly, nor standeth in the way
of sinners, nor sitteth in the seat of the scornful."

THE BODY OF CHRIST is full of definitions of what it means to be blessed. There is a false perception that having materials means you have the Blessing of the Lord.

The truth of what being blessed means is found in Psalm 1:1. By revelation, I know that God calls these things blessed because they open doors to a brighter future. By being counseled by the godly, you are getting God's viewpoints and His principals.

By not standing in the way of sinners, you are holding a standard of holiness.

If you say that you've accepted Jesus as your Lord and savior, a sinner should look at your life and be able to see that as truth. You should have to tell your testimony, not people be able to look at you and tell. Sitting in the seat of the scornful is you being self-righteous.

You're blessed when you lay your pride down and become
humble and are able to admit that if it had not been for the

Lord, you would still be bound.

Now that you've discovered what it truly means to be blessed, are you blessed, or do you just have a lot of stuff?

Let's focus on really being blessed so that the future of not only our lives, but this world will be brighter and the Kingdom of God can expand.

NOTES

Day 22
Atmosphere Changer

Matthew 5:13
"Ye are the salt of the earth; but if the salt have lost his savour, where with shall it be salted? It is thenceforth good for nothing, but to be cast out and to be trodden under the foot of men."

GOD CREATED YOU AND I to be atmosphere changers, not to be victims of circumstance. As an atmosphere changer, you have been given the authority by God to create what you want to see in any place.

Jesus understood this; when He ran across a blind man, He gave him sight.

If He ran across the hungry, He fed them.

The list goes on and on about how Jesus operated in His authority as an atmosphere changer.

My brothers and my sisters, change the atmosphere into an atmosphere that invites the presence of God in. Just like you would a thermostat in your home or car, turn it to the degree that comforts the presence of God. If you get to work and your boss is grumpy or co-workers have bad attitudes, do not fall victim of the demonic atmosphere.

CHANGE IT!

Change it so that you can flow in the Holy Ghost, be productive in your work, and effective in your walk with God!

NOTES

Day 23
Define Your Love By Giving

Acts 20:35
"I have shewed you all things, how that so laboring ye ought to support the weak, and to remember the words of the Lord Jesus, how he said, it is more Blessed to give than to receive."

IT'S EASY TO GET TRAPPED in the box of receiving. I say box because you limit yourself to how far you can really go when you confine yourself to only receiving and not defining yourself by your giving. You see, God himself defined how much He loved us by the giving of His only and begotten son. What you give and how much you give defines how valuable and important something is to you. A key to finding where your heart is, is to look at where you put your resources.

Where do you spend your time, money, and make your sacrifices?

Today, I want you to make a list of things that are important and valuable to you. Give into those things rather it be through volunteering your services, appreciation cards, or monetary sacrifices. Remember: You define the importance and value of something by your giving.

NOTES

JERRY WALKER

Day 24
Got Fruit?

Galatians 5:22-23
*"The fruit of the spirit is love, joy, peace,
longsuffering, gentleness, goodness, faith,
meekness, temperance..."*

IF YOU WERE TO STUDY FRUITS, whether it be apples, oranges, watermelons or strawberries, what you would find is that they all serve different purposes for the health and development of the body. They all hold different vitamins and nutrients that help the body function at its best and to grow to its fullest potential. As it is naturally, so it is spiritually. The fruit of the spirit, which is the character of God, helps our soul to function its best and grows in depth in God being made one with Him.

Think about how you react to circumstances and situations.

Are you bearing the Fruit of the Spirit?

Does your character look like the character of the Lord?

Today, bear fruit on purpose.

Think before you react so that you can respond with God's character. Show love when others disrespect you, have joy in tough moments, and stretch your faith out during discouraging circumstances.

When you begin to bear the "Fruit of the Spirit", God's will can be done in your life, and make your ways prosperous.

NOTES

Day 25
Answer the Call

Ephesians 4:11
"He gave some apostles, and some prophets, and some evangelists, and some pastors and teachers; for the perfecting of the saints, for the work of the ministry, for the edifying of the body of Christ."

GOD IS CALLING all His children to walk into their calling. Your calling is connected to your assignment. When you walk into your calling, it is for a much greater cause than yourself. The calling of God will bring clarity to the body of Christ making it whole. When everyone begins to function properly, *miracles, signs, and wonders* will follow.

Are you answering the call?

Life is full of opportunity and abundance.

Life opens up when you know who you are and why you were created. You can make a difference by answering your call and bringing light to the darkest parts of the world.

Today should be spent asking the Father, "What are you calling me to do?"

Time is valuable and you don't need to be going through life aimlessly. Your likes, dislikes, hopes, desires, struggles,

sensitivities are all leading you to your calling.
Answer it!

NOTES

Day 26
Put on the Whole Armor of God

Ephesians 6:11
"Put on the whole armor of God, that ye may be
able to stand against the wiles of the devil."

THE ARMOR OF GOD is very significant in your walk with God. It's what gives you the ability to say no to the devil. The Armor of God was designed to keep you in truth, righteousness, peace, faith, salvation and the word of God (read verses 14-17).

To reap the full benefits of wearing the Armor, you must consciously be aware that you have it on.

Believe it or not, the devil can't just come into our lives. We must give Him an invitation to come. When we are not consciously aware and alert, we often fall into the wiles of the enemy which causes him to possess territory in our lives.

Rehearse today Ephesians 6:11-17.

Really concentrate on what you are reading.

Write it down if you must. The more consciously aware you are about what you are doing, the less likely the devil will be able to gain territory and you can begin to live life and live it abundantly.

NOTES

_____
_____
_____
_____
_____
_____
_____
_____
_____
_____
_____
_____
_____
_____
_____
_____
_____
_____
_____
_____
_____
_____
_____
_____
_____
_____
_____

Day 27
Get the Lesson

Isaiah 30:20-21
"The Lord gives the bread of adversity and the
water of affliction, yet shall thy teachers be
removed into a corner anymore, but thine eyes
shall see thy teachers: And thine ears shall hear a
word behind the saying, this is the way, walk ye
in it, when ye turn to the right hand and when
ye turn to the left."

LIFE IS FULL OF DECISIONS. You make decision A to make decision B to end up making decision C. There will always be a decision to be made. Not all our decisions line up with the will of God for our lives. The above scripture lets us know that it is the Lord that gives adversity and affliction. The purpose for the adversity and affliction is so we can get back on the right path for our lives.

God is not punishing us for wrong decisions by holding His promises back.

Psalms 84:11(NIV) says, "For the Lord God is a sun and a shield; the Lord gives grace and Glory; no good thing does He withhold from those who walk uprightly (those who believe in the finished works of Christ)."

The foundational text also states, "Thine eyes shall see and thine ears shall hear." It's through us experiencing the pain of a decision that our senses become sensitive to God and his plan.

Where are you in life today? Are you making decisions outside the will of God? Is the Lord teaching you through adversity and affliction? By asking yourself these questions, I believe you will get back onto the path that God has set out for your life. Meditate before making decisions and seek godly counsel so that you won't make any wrong turns.

Wrong turns will come, but when the teacher shows up, GET THE LESSON!

NOTES

Day 28
The Blueprint

Psalm 1:1-3

"Blessed is the man that walketh not in the counsel of the ungodly, not standeth in the way of sinners, nor sitteth in the seat of the scornful. But his delight is in the law of the Lord; and in his law doth he meditate day and night. And he shall be like a tree planted by the rivers of water, that bringeth forth his fruit in his season; his leaf also shall not wither; and whatsoever he doeth shall prosper."

GOD DESIRES for each of His children is to be blessed and live prosperous and pleasurable lives. Job 36:11 tells us that, "If we obey and serve the Father, we will spend our days in prosperity and our years in pleasures."

I went out on a pursuit to define blessed: outside of consumerism and material gain, the Father gave me what I call the "Blessed Blueprint".

It has nothing to do with what you drive and the square footage of your home, or everything in it.

Being blessed means being holy and consecrated for the use of God and His Divine purpose.

Psalm 1:1-3 is how we do it!

I'm excited and happy for you. God's plan for you is not failure, misery, poverty, sickness, or disease. He has already set the blueprint for us to live blessed, helpful, integral, fruitful and prosperous.

NOTES

Day 29
What's the Time?

Ecclesiastes 3:1
"To everything there is a season, and a time for
every matter or purpose under heaven." (AMP)

HERE UNDER THE HEAVENS, it is always revolving. Its full of changes. There will be times to laugh and times to cry, times to plant and times to pluck up, times to sleep and times to awaken.

I submit to you today not to get attached to people, places, possessions, or positions. Always be ready to move with the Spirit. Yes, the world may be after stability, but our anchor is in the Lord.

What time is it in your life?

Maybe you're experiencing fulfillment, or maybe you're in a dark season. Whatever time it may be in your life, God wants to be a part of it. Allow the presence of God to be a part of it.

Allow the presence of God to be with you in all seasons and times. For where His spirit is, there is liberty.

NOTES

Day 30
Forgiveness

Matthew 6:14-15
"For if ye forgive men of their trespasses, your heavenly father will also forgive you. But if ye forgive not men of their trespasses, neither will your father forgive your trespasses."

WHEN WE FORGIVE OTHERS, our Heavenly Father can forgive us. Through my own walk of forgiveness, I've learned that I can forgive the person, but not the act.

Ephesians 6:12 lets us know that our struggle is not against flesh and blood, but against operations of the kingdom of darkness.

So when I forgive a person, I know and understand that they are human and fall short of the Glory of God.

Being a Child of God, there should be enough wisdom in us to be against the action and not tolerate or allow it again.

Love the person and hate the behavior.

NOTES

Day 31
Self-Discovery

Daniel 11:32
*".... But the people that do know their God shall
be strong, and do exploits."*

OFTEN WE CAN GET into a certain pattern or routine, and stay in what I call "Black and White Mode." God wants us to step out and do something unexpected. He wants us to do daring deeds. Do something that others— even yourself, thought that you couldn't do. I believe God our Father wants us to do exploits so that we can learn our abilities, talents, gifts, and so that we never fully peak and provoke others to want to discover their capacities.

Discovery of self-discovery is the best discovery.

I dare you to do a daring deed today! Do something unexpected. If you're a singer, put the mic down and write. If you play the drums, drop the sticks and pick up a guitar. If you're a cook, try gardening. These are just a few ideas to get you started. There is more to you than what you've already discovered.

NOTES

About the Author

JERRY WALKER is a Kingdom Ambassador with an assignment to transform mediocre minds into Christ mentalities. Born in a poverty-stricken single parent home with no opportunity and few possibilities, Walker has followed the precepts from scripture to live a life of total Victory!

J. Kenkade
PUBLISHING®

Transforming Life Stories

Ready to Get Published?

Our All-Inclusive Publishing Package

Professional Proofreading & Editing
Interior Design & Cover Design
Manuscript Writing Assistance
Affordable Pricing & More

For Manuscript Submission or other inquiries:
www.jkenkade.com
(501) 482-JKEN

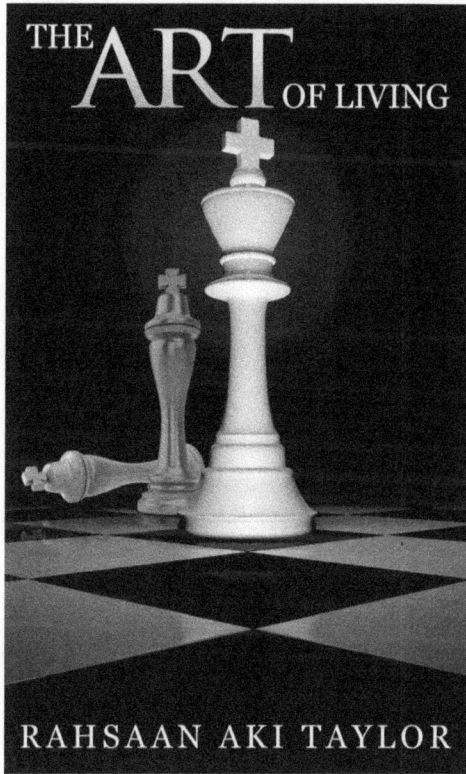

Also Available from J. Kenkade Publishing

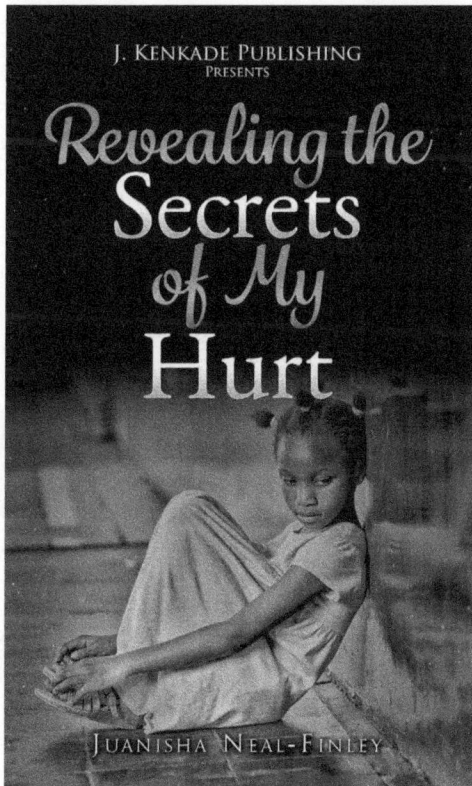

ISBN: 978-1-944486-13-6
Purchase at www.jkenkade.com

Captivating. Step into the life story of a young girl tormented by an abusive family. Young Cindy rewrites her experiences with a mother introduced to drugs, sexual abuse from her father, and death. Cindy reveals how strong God can make anyone in the midst of Satan's schemes. Experience her journey in "Revealing the Secrets of My Hurt."

Also Available from
J. Kenkade Publishing

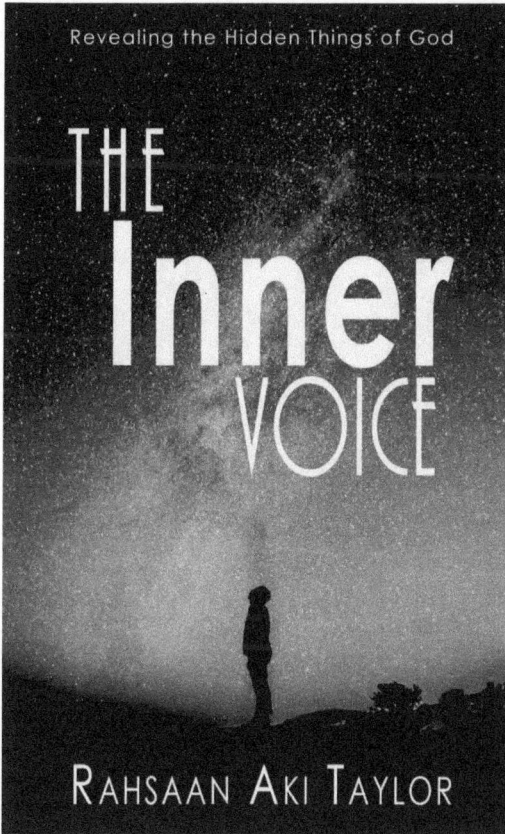

Revealing the Hidden Things of God

THE Inner VOICE

RAHSAAN AKI TAYLOR

ISBN: 978-1-944486-12-9
Purchase at www.jkenkade.com

We all have wondered why bad things happen to us or someone we love. Often times, we never receive the answer to the questions that are asked. Therefore, the content of this book will expose the unknown. It is guaranteed to have you on the edge of your seat. It teaches how to prevent failures and mishaps and will reveal some of the hidden things of God.

www.ingramcontent.com/pod-product-compliance
Lightning Source LLC
Chambersburg PA
CBHW021127020426
42331CB00005B/655